Heinemann

Britain in the
Age of Total War

1939-45

MALCOLM CHANDLER

Heinemann Educational Publishers
Halley Court, Jordan Hill, Oxford, OX2 8EJ
a division of Reed Educational & Professional
Publishing Ltd
Heinemann is a registered trademark of Reed
Educational & Professional Publishing Ltd

OXFORD MELBOURNE AUCKLAND
JOHANNESBURG BLANTYRE GABORONE
IBADAN PORTSMOUTH NH (USA) CHICAGO

First published 2002

ISBN 0 435 32730 5
04 03 02 01
10 9 8 7 6 5 4 3 2 1
Designed and typeset by Jonathan Williams
Printed and bound in Spain by Edelvives
Picture research by Liz Moore

Photographic acknowledgements
The author and publisher would like to thank the
following for permission to reproduce photographs:
Hulton Archive: 9B, 10C, 13A, 16B, 16D, 20C, 22G, 30D
Hulton Getty: 3A, 6B, 8A
Popperfoto: 15A 28B, 29C
Public Record Office: 24J
Topham Picturepoint: 11E
Cover photograph: © Popperfoto

Britain in the Age of Total War 1939–45

Contents

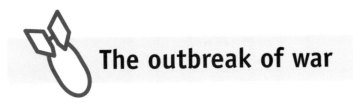

The outbreak of war

At 11.45 am on the morning of 3 September 1939, the programme on the BBC radio was interrupted for a special broadcast by the Prime Minister, Neville Chamberlain. He spoke from 10 Downing Street and announced that Britain and Germany had been at war since 11.00 am that morning.

To most people in Britain the news that war had been declared came as no surprise, as it had been expected for many months. In fact war had almost broken out in September 1938 at the time of the Munich Crisis. On 15 September 1938 Hitler had demanded self-determination for the Sudeten Germans in western Czechoslovakia. Chamberlain agreed to his demands. At a second meeting with Hitler on 22 September 1938, Hitler told Chamberlain that he wanted the whole of the Sudetenland, so when Chamberlain returned to Britain he ordered preparations for an immediate outbreak of hostilities. Trenches were dug, air-raid shelters were constructed and plans for evacuation were started. The government appealed for 1 million volunteers to serve in the emergency. In fact by 1 November, 5 million people had volunteered to serve in the Civil Defence.

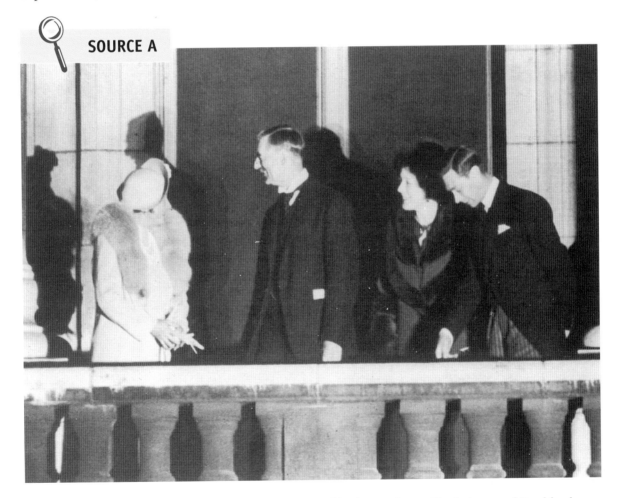

SOURCE A

▲ Prime Minister Neville Chamberlain and his wife (centre), on the balcony of Buckingham Palace with the king and queen, 30 September 1938.

The prospect of war disappeared after Chamberlain signed the Munich Agreement and the Anglo-German Agreement on 29 and 30 September 1938. Hitler was allowed to occupy the Sudetenland and Czechoslovakia lost its coalfields and its defences. Chamberlain returned in triumph to a hero's welcome. He announced that it was 'Peace in our time', and appeared on the balcony of Buckingham Palace with King George VI and Queen Elizabeth (see Source A). But within six months all hope of peace began to disappear.

In March 1939 Hitler occupied the rest of Bohemia and Moravia, the remainder of western Czechoslovakia. This was a clear violation of the Munich Agreement and showed that Hitler's aims went beyond just uniting all German speakers in a Greater Germany.

In April 1939, in response to Hitler's actions, Britain made defensive alliances with Romania and Poland. These meant that if either country were attacked, Britain would go to war to defend it. For the first time Britain introduced conscription in peacetime and men of twenty and twenty-one years of age were required to undergo six months of military training.

Throughout the spring and summer of 1939, Britain and France attempted to form an alliance with the Soviet Union, but, after a series of delays, Stalin signed the Nazi-Soviet Pact with Hitler on 23 August 1939.

On the face of it the Nazi-Soviet Pact was a simple non-aggression pact between the two countries in that they both agreed not to attack each other. But Hitler and Stalin had been bitter enemies and the agreement astounded politicians throughout Europe. Stalin was terrified that Hitler would attack the Soviet Union and wanted to prevent it at all costs.

Chamberlain's reaction to the Nazi-Soviet Pact was to sign a further alliance with Poland on 25 August. This was intended to be a warning to Hitler not to invade, but it failed. By then Hitler did not believe that Chamberlain would intervene to help Poland. And so, on 1 September 1939, Germany invaded Poland. On 2 September 1939 the British government sent an ultimatum to Germany demanding that all forces should be withdrawn from Poland or war would be declared. The German government was ordered to reply by 11 am on 3 September. This was ignored, and so, on 3 September 1939, Britain declared war on Germany.

What effects did the Munich Crisis have?

The war scare in September 1938 at the time of the Munich Crisis had provided valuable practice for a real war. In addition, since September 1938, gas masks had been produced for everybody in the population and many air raid shelters had been constructed. The most widely used air raid shelter was the Anderson shelter, made of corrugated metal, which was produced in large numbers and dug into back gardens all over Britain. Eventually more than 2 million were made available.

More important for the survival of Britain was the completion of the radar network along the east and south coasts of Britain. Radar had been invented by Robert Watson Watt in 1936, but the stations were only completed in the summer of 1939. They gave the RAF vital warning of German air raids. The RAF itself also benefited from the eleven-month delay between Munich and the outbreak of war. The two fighters that were to play such a crucial role in the Battle of Britain, the Spitfire and the Hurricane, had only just taken to the air in 1938. By 1940 they would now be available in sufficient numbers to take on the more numerous Luftwaffe (the German airforce).

How did the British government react at the outbreak of war?

It had been widely assumed throughout the 1930s that a Second World War would result in casualties on a massive scale. The British government's main concern, therefore, was to try to prevent civilian casualties as far as possible but at the same time prepare for the worst.

To reduce the risk of casualties, people were ordered to stay off the streets and all cinemas and theatres were closed. Strict air raid precautions were put in force. All houses had to have blackout over all windows so that no light could be seen from outside and they had to be taped up to prevent accidents from flying glass. Car headlights were to be switched off and traffic lights were covered to reduce the glare. It became an offence to be seen without a gas mask.

A series of regulations came into force which were designed to prevent a successful German invasion. Church bells were to be kept silent, unless an invading force landed. Emergency transport had to be listed, and that included handcarts and horses, as well as cars and lorries. All wells, springs, ponds and rivers were listed so that a water supply could be found and used in emergencies.

Evacuation

The most organised reaction to the outbreak of war was evacuation. Children and other vulnerable people were moved from areas that were likely to be bombed (such as large cities). Britain was divided into three regions: Evacuation Areas, Neutral Areas and Reception Areas. People at risk were moved from Evacuation Areas to Reception Areas in one four-day period from 1 to 4 September. The whole transport system was taken over for this.

Evacuees consisted of children, their teachers, pregnant women and the elderly. Altogether about 1.4 million people were evacuated. Children were allowed to take one suitcase and had labels around their necks in case they got lost. In the reception areas host families were allowed to choose the evacuees they wanted to house.

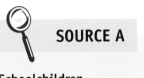

SOURCE A	
Schoolchildren	827,000
Mothers and children	524,000
Pregnant women	13,000
Blind and disabled people	7,000
Teachers	103,000

▲ Number of people evacuated in September 1939.

What effects did evacuation have upon people in Britain?

Evacuation led to a complete mixing of social classes. Children from middle-class families were sent to live with working-class families and vice versa. This was not always successful. The mixture of people from town and country produced friction on many occasions, but there was also a positive effect. For almost the first time the true state of children from the poorest areas of Britain, the inner cities, became widely known. Many people were horrified at the state of health of these evacuees. In 1941 the Women's Institute compiled a report on the health of evacuees and listed the problems that they suffered from (see Source C).

Many children were not used to an inside toilet, running water, carpets, baths; they often did not change their clothes regularly and were infested with lice or were suffering from skin diseases like impetigo (an infectious skin disease which causes ulcers).

▲ **Children at Ealing Broadway Station in London, 2 September 1939, some of the first to be evacuated.**

On the other hand, the impact of life in the country and better food was soon apparent.

SOURCE C

The state of the children was such that the school had to be fumigated [disinfected using smoke and fumes].

The children were filthy. We have never seen so many verminous [dirty, like vermin] *children lacking any knowledge of clean habits. They had not had a bath for months.*

One child was suffering from scabies [an infectious skin disease caused by mites], *the majority had it in their hair, and the others had dirty septic sores all over their bodies.*

Some of the children were sent in their ragged little garments. Most of the children were walking on the ground, their shoes had no soles and just uppers hanging together.

Many of the mothers and children were bed-wetters.

Extracts from a report published by the Women's Institute in 1941.

Reports like these played an important part in convincing the government and public opinion that major social reforms would be needed at the end of the war. The evidence of evacuation was a major factor in the decision to set up the Beveridge Commission in 1941. The aim of the commission was to suggest ways in which life in Britain could be improved after the war (see pages 25-7).

The phoney war

The government's worst fears did not materialise in September 1939. There were no air raids and no casualties. The British Expeditionary Force (BEF) that set off for Belgium saw no action in the final months of 1939 nor the beginning of 1940, and for a time it appeared that the predictions of devastation were not going to come true. As a result, the British people began to relax and forget many of the new regulations. Evacuation, which had never been popular with many parents and was not compulsory, proved increasingly difficult to maintain. Many evacuees had returned home by Christmas and life appeared to be getting back to normal. All cinemas and theatres were reopened in December 1939.

This was known as the 'Phoney War', or the 'Bore War', as nothing seemed to be happening. In many ways it was disastrous for the British government and its attempt to impose regulations on the people of Britain, as it made it much harder to enforce regulations when the real crisis began in 1940.

Rationing

One form of regulation that was taken seriously during the Phoney War was rationing, which began in January 1940 and continued throughout the war. At first only butter, sugar and bacon were rationed, but clothing, soap and petrol were all added in 1941. Some forms of rationing lasted until 1953. Some foods, notably bread, were rationed only after the end of the war.

To help people to use less of the rationed goods the government introduced a number of initiatives. The 'Make-do and Mend' campaign encouraged people to save on material by mending their own clothes. The utility mark on cheaper, more basic clothing and furniture showed that by buying these goods people were helping the war effort. Finally, to save fuel many people stopped using their cars and the government encouraged people to use less hot water.

Why was rationing introduced?

The main purpose of rationing was to ensure that there were adequate supplies of food for the British people. During the First World War the Germans had attempted to starve Britain through its U-boat campaign. By 1939 Britain imported over half of its food supply. Another submarine attack on Britain's trade routes could spell disaster.

Rationing was also an attempt to ensure that food supplies in Britain were divided up as equally as possible, and so helping most of the population stay healthy. This had two purposes: not only would people be fit to work, but they would also need little hospital care or other medical treatment. Both of these would help the war effort tremendously as there were bound to be many urgent casualties from bombing.

Foods that were rationed

Sweets, Meat, Butter, Jam, Cheese, Fats, Bacon, Tea, Eggs, Dried milk, Dried eggs

Foods that were not

Vegetables, Bread, Potatoes, Fish, Milk (actually milk was rationed, but the milk ration was 3 pints a week and this was an increase for most people)

How was rationing implemented?

Everyone was issued with a ration book containing coupons for goods and had to register with a butcher and a grocer. These shopkeepers were then supplied with enough food for their customers. People also had to take their ration books with them if they went on holiday.

Special supplements were made available for young children, such as orange juice and cod liver oil. The government also encouraged people to use alternatives to rationed goods, such as powdered milk or spam (Supply Pressed American Meat).

To help families even further, school meals were made available for every child so that mothers could work during the day and not have to worry about their children at lunchtime. When rationing was first introduced more wealthy people tried to avoid the coupon system by eating in restaurants. But from 1942 restaurants were not allowed to charge more than the equivalent of 25p for a meal (about a few pounds today).

What were the consequences of rationing?

During the war some people's diets improved. This was partly because the government wanted people to eat healthily but also because poorer people could now afford to buy better food.

In the long run rationing had a profound effect on government policy. Before, many politicians believed that it was impossible to make major changes to the nation's health. Some did not even believe that it was the government's responsibility. But as a result of rationing, the government took responsibility for the welfare of all the people of Britain for the first time and the results were startling. By 1941 consumption of potatoes had risen by

40 per cent, vegetables by 30 per cent and milk by 30 per cent.

'Dig for Victory'

To try to grow extra food, more than 50 per cent of working people began to keep allotments. These were part of the 'Dig for Victory' campaign that encouraged people to grow as much of their own food as possible. By 1943 there were 1.4 million allotments in Britain.

People also tried to buy food and other things that were difficult to get hold of by buying goods on the 'black market'. These were sold at high prices by traders or 'under the counter' in shops.

SOURCE A

▲ A gardener tending vegetables in allotments dug in the moat of the Tower of London, June 1940.

Total war

The Second World War is described as a 'total war' because it affected both civilians at home and in their everyday lives and soldiers fighting at the front.

The Phoney War ended when Germany invaded Denmark and Norway in April 1940. The German invasion of Holland, Belgium and France followed in May 1940. In the midst of the attacks, Neville Chamberlain resigned as Prime Minister and was replaced by Winston Churchill, who formed a coalition government of all political parties.

Dunkirk, May–June 1940

At first Churchill was under great pressure from other members of the Cabinet, especially Lord Halifax, to make peace with Hitler. Churchill resisted all the pressure, but could do nothing to help the British Expeditionary

Force, which found itself outflanked and cut off. It was forced to retreat onto the beaches of Calais and Dunkirk and between 27 May and 4 June 1940 some 340,000 men were rescued by the Royal Navy and hundreds of small privately owned boats in 'Operation Dynamo'.

 **SOURCE A**

All night and all day men of the undefeated British Expeditionary Force have been coming home. From interviews with the men it is clear they have come back in glory; that their morale is as high as ever, and that they are anxious to be back again 'to have a real crack at Jerry [the Germans]'.

Extract from the news on the BBC Home Service, 31 May 1940.

SOURCE B

▲ **Ships carrying members of the BEF leaving Dunkirk, June 1940.**

Newspapers published stories about the 'Miracle of Dunkirk' and one carried the headline 'Bloody Marvellous'. This gave rise to the 'Dunkirk Spirit': the idea that Britain could stand the test and would win through. But the truth was somewhat different. The BEF had lost a large amount of equipment: 475 tanks, 1000 heavy guns and 400 anti-tank guns.

The impact of Dunkirk hit very hard. The BEF casualties totalled 68,000. Survivors were warned not to discuss the incident when they returned home. This was one of the first times that the government tried to censor the news. Also, so much equipment had been lost that it became impossible for Britain to defend France.

After Dunkirk the situation became much worse. Within a month of the evacuation of Dunkirk, France collapsed and surrendered in the second half of June and Britain had to fight on its own against German armed forces. In southern France, Germany allowed a government to be set up at Vichy which was run by General Pétain. The Vichy government was really controlled by Germans.

Conscription had not yet produced fully trained men so Winston Churchill set up the Local Defence Volunteers, which soon became known as the Home Guard.

Members of the Home Guard trained every night, and often at weekends, from June 1940 until the end of 1944. The members could not match the skill and expertise of fully trained soldiers, but they could relieve the regular army of many of its more routine duties, such as patrols, guard duty and escorts for prisoners of war.

SOURCE C

▲ **Fishermen on Holy Island, off the north-east coast of England, learning how to use rifles as part of their Home Guard training.**

However, by the summer of 1940 the possibility of a German invasion seemed very real indeed.

SOURCE D

Such a force is of the highest value and importance. A country where every street and every village bristles with resolute armed men is a country which would not be able to be overthrown.

Extract from a speech about the Home Guard, made by Winston Churchill, November 1940.

The Battle of Britain

After the fall of France on 22 June 1940, Hitler turned his attention to Britain. The German aim was simple: they wanted to destroy the RAF as a prelude to the invasion of Britain in 'Operation Sealion'. The first attacks in July were on shipping in the Channel, then the Luftwaffe began to bomb ports, airfields and radar stations. Finally, from the middle of August, came a prolonged battle in the skies over Britain. This was the Battle of Britain.

At first the RAF was more than equal to the challenge as more enemy aircraft were shot down than were lost. But after several weeks the tide began to turn and the RAF began to lose more aircraft. In fact it was not the aircraft that were the key to the situation, it was the pilots. Industry was able to replace the planes, but it took longer to train pilots. Soon pilots were going into the air with only ten hours flying experience and then taking off as many as seven times a day, if they survived. But without warning, Hitler changed his tactics.

On 7 September Hitler ordered an end to daylight attacks on RAF airfields and sent the Luftwaffe on night-time attacks on London and other cities. This was known as the Blitz.

SOURCE E

▲ A painting of RAF Spitfires attacking German bombers during the Battle of Britain.

In the first attack 617 fighters escorted 348 bombers across the Channel and then protected them while they dropped their bombs on London Docks, the Woolwich Arsenal and the armaments factories at Silvertown. The RAF was taken by surprise and the bombers were able to take their time to pick their targets. By dawn 430 Londoners were dead and 1600 were injured.

The switch from attacks on the RAF to night-time raids on British cities allowed the RAF to rest and recover. The Battle of Britain had been won.

Operation Sealion was called off on 17 September. Instead the Germans began a prolonged night-time attack on British cities which lasted until the summer of 1941.

The Blitz

The aim of the Blitz was to break the morale of the British people by destroying their homes.

The Blitz was also an attempt to destroy transport and industry. In London the docks were attacked regularly and across Britain the Luftwaffe also tried to hit railway lines and junctions, power stations and ports.

During September 1940 London was bombed almost every night. The Germans dropped an average of 250 tonnes of bombs each time (approximately the same as the total number of bombs dropped on Britain throughout the First World War).

The Blitz of 1940 was very difficult, as bombing destroyed homes, lives and families. Every major town and city in the British Isles was attacked. The worst affected city was London, where 13,000 people were killed in 1940. By the summer of 1941 there had been 43,000 people killed in air raids across Britain.

On 10 September a bomb hit Buckingham Palace, while the king and queen were at Windsor, but on 13 September the Palace was bombed while the king and queen were in residence. The idea that the Royal Family was

SOURCE A

Our main assignments now were the disturbance of production and incoming supplies. The underlying purpose was to slow down British armament production and begin a full-scale economic war. To destroy civilian morale we began 'reprisal raids' at the same time.

Field Marshal Kesselring explained the aims of the German air attacks in his memoirs, written in 1957.

SOURCE B

The whole story of the last weekend has been one of unplanned hysteria. The newspaper versions of life going on normally in the East End are greatly distorted. There was no bread, no milk, no telephones. There is no humour or laughter. There was thus every excuse for people to be distressed. There was no understanding in the huge government buildings of central London for the tiny crumbled streets of massed populations.

Extract from a report produced by local government officials in the East End of London in September 1940.

suffering as well as the people of the East End of London somehow made a difference, even though the damage to Buckingham Palace was slight. The Royal Family announced that it would be staying in the Palace throughout the war. This sent a clear message of solidarity to the rest of London and Britain.

While newspapers, which were all controlled by government censorship (see pages 14–15), printed stories of high morale and 'Britain can take it', unofficial reports suggested that people were in despair.

Civilians at war

Despite heavy losses in other British cities, the worst effects of the Blitz were felt by the people of London. In September, October and November 1940 there appeared to be no way of stopping the German bombers, although the use of radar gave warnings of attacks. The results of the bombing raids were the destruction of large areas of the East End of London and many civilian casualties.

Despite the two million Anderson shelters that were produced in the early years of the war, many people had no shelters, particularly those living in city centres or in flats. Some moved in with friends or relatives during raids, others moved onto the ground floor. Here they constructed a safe room, sometimes in a cellar. Some people used a Morrison shelter, which was a steel cage that fitted under a dining table.

SOURCE A

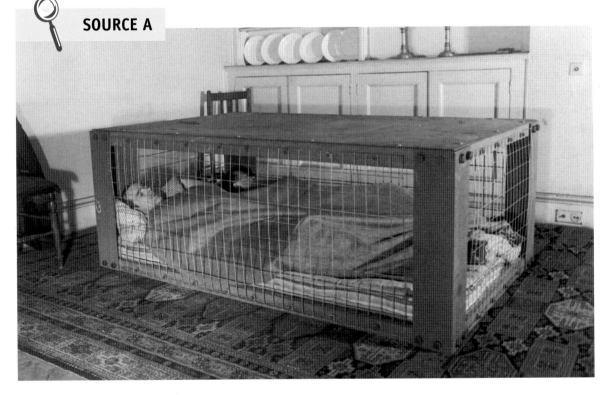

▲ **Men sleeping in a Morrison shelter, set up their living room in London, September 1940. The cage sides were designed to stop broken shards hitting the occupants if the building was bombed.**

Many people also took to sheltering in the Underground. About 150,000 people did so every night. Even so, only about 4 per cent of Londoners used the Underground for shelter at night; 60 per cent of people stayed in their own homes throughout the war.

Air-raid wardens

The task of tackling the effects of bombing fell to the emergency services, which were backed up by volunteers. When a bomb landed it would be reported to the local Air Raid Precaution (ARP) post. There would usually be six wardens at each post covering about five hundred people. During the day their job was to check that the ARP regulations were being obeyed and at night they inspected blackout precautions and then reported raids. The ARP wardens would then alert other emergency services, such as the Fire Service, which was supported by the volunteers in the Auxiliary Fire Service.

Their task could be overwhelming. On the nights of 7, 18 and 24 September 1940 there were more than 1000 fires in London alone, many caused by small incendiary bombs. These bombs burst into flames and could cause huge damage and were often far more dangerous than high explosive bombs. All large buildings were supposed to have fire-watchers, who could put out incendiaries by pouring sand over them, but this only applied to buildings that employed more than 30 people. The result was that there were many fires that could have been avoided.

How were the ARP regulations enforced?

The Air Raid Precaution wardens were the key people in making sure that Britain was as safe as possible at night. They had the job of checking every house. There had to be a 'safe room', where the people would be sheltering, proper blackout, a pump and bucket of sand. Wardens also had to be told how many people were sleeping in each house each night. This would enable them to co-ordinate a rescue the following day. Heavy Rescue Squads did not want to waste time looking for people who had not been in the house the night before. The fine for breaking blackout regulations could be as much as £150, followed by imprisonment.

At first ARP wardens were often regarded as 'nosey parkers', because they asked questions about people's private lives and could search houses. But as the dangers of bombing grew they came to be accepted. About one in six of wardens were women, many combining a job and family life with their duties.

The effects of wartime bombing

After the first big raids on London on 7 and 8 September, Churchill immediately realised the importance of maintaining the morale of the British people, and so keeping their spirits high.

Censorship and propaganda

The most obvious way of controlling the news was through censorship. The Ministry of Information was the government department responsible for informing people about events in the war as well as keeping up morale. The government had given itself the power to stop any news being published that it did not like. Any photographs that were likely to undermine public morale were withheld. These were photographs that showed large numbers of casualties, or serious damage. A photograph taken of a school playground in

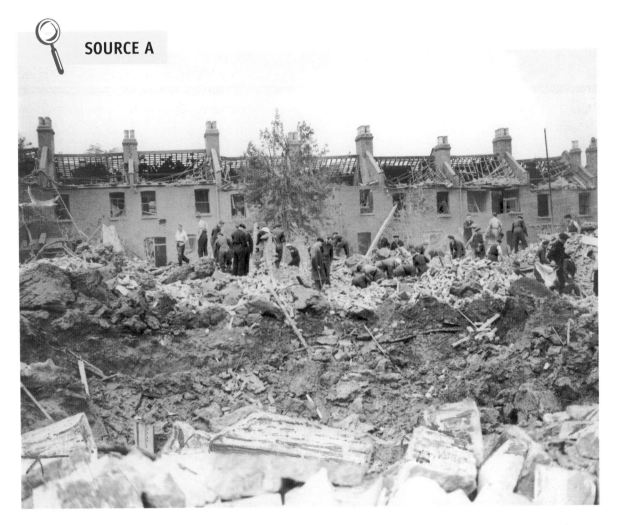

▲ This type of photograph, showing extensive bomb damage, would have been censored.
This shows a crater and damaged houses in Hoe Street, Walthamstow, 14 September 1944.

Catford, London, was withheld because it showed dead children, as were photographs of angry people or looting. In addition government officials checked written documents, films and photographs to ensure that they did not contain any information which the enemy might find useful.

On the other hand, photographs of defiance and heroism were put on the front pages of newspapers. The most famous example was the picture of St Paul's Cathedral surrounded by flames in December 1940 (Source B). Only recently did it come to light that this photograph had actually been partly faked. Clouds and flames had been added to the original to make it look more dramatic.

Newspaper articles were also restricted. Any references to panic or hysteria were immediately removed. Source C is a report of the raid on Coventry on 14 November 1940 which was not seen by the public.

This report described the effects of one of the most devastating raids of the war. Coventry was hit with great precision and four thousand people were killed in a raid lasting ten hours. One third of the city was damaged (see Source D). Many people began 'trekking' to avoid further danger. This meant that families moved out into the countryside every night and slept in fields to escape any further attacks.

▲ St Paul's Cathedral, seen through smoke and flames, December 1940.

SOURCE C

There were more open signs of hysteria and terror than observed in the previous two months. The overwhelming feeling on Friday was the feeling of utter helplessness. The tremendous impact of the previous night had left many people speechless. On Friday evening (15 November), there were several signs of suppressed panic as darkness approached.

Extract from an official report into events after the bombing of Coventry on 14 November 1940.

SOURCE D

▲ Extensive bomb damage in Coventry, November 1940.

As the war progressed the government used radio, cinema and newspapers as key tools in maintaining morale and helping the British people to fight on with determination. Letters like that in Source E were only too welcome.

SOURCE E

What warmth – what courage! What determination. People singing in public shelters. WVS (Women's Voluntary Service) girls serving hot drinks to fire-fighters during raids. Everyone secretly delighted with the privilege of holding up Hitler. Certain of beating him.

Extract from a letter by Humphrey Jennings, October 1940.

Humphrey Jennings was part of the government's attempts to build up morale. He was a film maker employed by the Ministry of Information. He not only produced many films advising people about the regulations, but part of his work was also to make films that would inspire people to want to continue the fight. They publicised the work of volunteers and described what life would be like when the war was won to help overcome the demoralising effects of continued bombing.

Documentary films were made in order to keep the nation as informed as possible and radio was used increasingly for spreading information but also as a way of keeping up morale. Many comedy programmes were made such as *It's That Man Again*, which poked fun at Hitler, the Germans and the British. By 1945 more than ten million people owned what was then called a wireless (radio).

The Germans also used radio as part of their propaganda. Radio Hamburg could be picked up in Britain and broadcasts by William Joyce could be heard. He was born in the USA but moved to England in 1922. He sympathised with Nazi views, however, so moved to Germany before the war broke out.

During the war his broadcasts mocked the British war effort, to the extent that people nicknamed him 'Lord Haw Haw'. After the war he was brought back to Britain, found guilty of treason and hanged.

Radio, films and poster campaigns not only kept people informed about events but also encouraged people to save to help the war effort. Public information leaflets were produced to tell people what action to take, for instance during a gas attack. Finally, the press was used for recruitment, for instance for men to join the Home Guard, or women to join the factories.

What effects did bombing have on industry?

From November 1940, the Luftwaffe began to concentrate its bombing on British cities other than London. This was a sign that in addition to its attempts to break the morale of the British people it was also beginning to focus more on industry. The raid on Coventry was the most devastating. But there were also severe raids on many major cities, such as Canterbury, Birmingham, Bristol, Southampton, Manchester and Sheffield. Some attempts to attack Belfast ended with bombs being dropped on Dublin, which was in neutral Eire, where there was no blackout.

Bombing of industrial targets was less effective because more precision was needed. Factories, unlike housing estates, were sometimes isolated and could easily be missed at night. As a result, most German bombing was indiscriminate and failed to put industry out of action. Most factories were able to resume production within two to three days of being hit.

Bombing continued on a lesser scale throughout the winter of 1940–1 and then began again in the early spring. Ports were raided again and again. By January 1941, there had been 530 people killed in Southampton and 1000 in Bristol. On 2 January, Cardiff was hit by a raid of 125 bombers and 299 people died.

The naval base at Portsmouth was the target for a massive attack on 10 January 1941. There were 930 civilians killed and almost 3000 injured. Naval casualties were never revealed. An official report described an almost complete breakdown of morale and law and order (see Source F). It was never published.

At Easter 1941, Belfast was attacked for the first time and more than 900 people were killed in the 'Belfast Blitz'. The city and its

SOURCE F

By 6.00 pm all traffic is moving northwards. The movement begins at 3.30 pm and continues to dusk. The people are making for the bridge on the main road out of Portsmouth in order to sleep in the northern suburbs, the surrounding hills, or towns and villages in the radius of twenty miles. One night it was estimated that 90,000 people left the city.

Looting and wanton destruction have reached alarming proportions. The police seem unable to exercise control. The effect on morale is bad and there is a general feeling of desperation as there seems to be no solution.

Extract from an official report into the effects of the bombing of Portsmouth on 10 January 1941.

defences were caught largely unawares and unprotected. From May 1941, however, the number of attacks on Britain began to drop. The Luftwaffe withdrew aircraft from France and moved them east in preparation for the invasion of the Soviet Union, which eventually began on 22 June. By then Britain had survived the worst of the Blitz, but over 40,000 civilians had been killed. Although this was far fewer than the government had originally expected, it was still a major sacrifice on the part of the British people.

The Luftwaffe continued to raid British cities from 1941 to 1944, but the attacks became less and less frequent as Allied air power increased. From December 1941 the RAF began to be supported by the United States Army Air Force (USAAF) and by 1944 the Allies had almost total air superiority. When the D-Day landings took place in June 1944, the Allies were able to put 10,000 planes into the air over the Normandy beaches.

V1s and V2s

In 1944 and 1945 Britain was attacked from the air once again. The first attacks came from pilotless rocket planes called V1s. These flying bombs or 'doodlebugs', as they became known, were frightening weapons. People on the ground could hear the engine cut out and then a shriek as the bomb hurtled to the ground. They brought a return to the days of the Blitz four years earlier.

From 13 June to 1 September 1944, some 2204 V1s fell on London and its suburbs. The worst hit areas were to the south and east of the city. At the same time, 1444 flying bombs landed in Kent, 880 in Sussex, 412 in Essex and 295 in Surrey. V2s were a much more serious threat and were fired from sites in Holland. They could not be shot down and there was no defence against them as they landed without any warning. The attacks were only stopped when the launch sites were overrun in 1945.

While in general British morale was not broken by the Blitz, it still served as the most terrifying ordeal for thousands of British civilians.

The role of women during the Second World War

Unlike in the First World War, at the beginning of the Second World War the government quickly realised that women could play an important part in the war effort. All women under the age of 40 were classified as 'mobile' or 'immobile'. Mobile meant that they were capable of joining the armed forces or of undertaking full-time war work. Immobile meant that they were housewives looking after children or elderly relatives.

Women were soon fully involved in many aspects of war work. Mobile women worked in Royal Ordnance factories, the Land Army and the Civil Defence. Many immobile women registered for voluntary work with organisations such as the Women's Voluntary Service (WVS), but others had part-time work in industry.

There were constant appeals in the press and in poster campaigns for women to help in industry. 'Come into the factories' was a slogan that appeared everywhere.

Women were soon employed in aircraft factories, where they could work a sixteen-hour day seven days a week, without any bank holidays. Many also worked in munitions factories. Others worked as mechanics, lorry drivers and engineers. All women received lower pay than men doing the same work. They also found that the National Insurance Act and the Personal Injuries Act (which gave workers compensation for injuries at work) discriminated against them.

SOURCE A

Did you know that over 10,000 women are doing men's work on one of Britain's railways alone? They are acting as plate-layers and permanent way labourers, helping with maintenance work, clerks, ticket collectors, porters, etc.

Go to it!

Want a job to stick to? Then try bill-posting! Bravo the women flight mechanics! Ever thought of yourself as an electrician? Be a welder.

Come into the factories!

An appeal that appeared in 1940.

Women also began to assume many of the responsibilities for the new regulations (see page 14). Evacuation was largely organised and operated by women, and they also took over the precautions for the blackout. When rationing was introduced in January 1940, it was women who had to organise the family budget and try to make the most of what food was available. Coming up with a variety of meals from basically the same ingredients week after week was a very difficult task, but was vital if morale was to be maintained.

Conscription of women

The work of women was not properly organised by the government until 1941. In April of that year all women were forced to register for work, but the real change was brought about by a report published by the Ministry of Labour in October 1941. This showed that two million more workers were needed in the armed forces and war industries. In December 1941 conscription of women aged 19 to 30 was introduced. From then on the number of women involved in the war effort steadily increased. By 1943 some 17 million women aged between 14 and 64 were either in the forces or in essential war work. That included 90 per cent of single women and 80 per cent of married women with children over 14.

Factory work

By 1943 women had proved that the war could not be won without their efforts. The value of their contribution to the war effort was unquestioned. They occupied 57 per cent of the jobs in factories, and, when they were in direct competition with men, often showed that they could do better. The Ministry of Information published details of women's achievements. A woman welder produced 'thirty feet more than a man on similar work'. A woman in a munitions factory 'produced 120 pieces of equipment a day, compared to 100 by her male colleagues'.

SOURCE B

Working in factories is not fun. To be shut in for hours on end without even a window to see daylight was grim. The noise was terrific and at night when you shut your eyes to sleep all the noise would start again in your head. Night shifts were the worst. The work was very often monotonous. I think boredom was our worst enemy.

One woman worker describing her experiences in 1942.

SOURCE C

▲ **A woman working in a munitions factory making shells, 1944.**

Often, however, the work was monotonous and boring (see Source B).

There were many other problems related to factory work. Many of the women working in factories faced a twelve-hour day. The factories were also usually a long way from home because they were often built in remote areas, such as Cumbria, to avoid the risk of bombing. Travel could be very difficult and expensive. Pay for women was also lower than for men, usually about 75 per cent of a man's wage (see below).

Average weekly earnings July 1943		
Men over 21 years	121s 4d	(£6.07)
Men under 21 years	47s 11d	(£2.40)
Women over 18 years	62s 11d	(£3.30)
Women part-time workers	29s 0d	(£1.45)
Women under 18 years	33s 11d	(£1.70)

Women complained because they did not receive enough money from the government while their husbands were serving in the armed forces. The lowest ranks in the forces were paid only two shillings a day in 1939 – 70p a week in today's terms. A wife with two children received a weekly allowance of £1.25 at a time when wages ranged from £3 to £10. Not until 1943 were wives of servicemen paid a War Service Grant of £3 a week. Figures from the Ministry of Labour in 1943 bore out some of the women's grievances.

The work of women factory workers was, however, recognised by the government. An Equal Pay Commission was set up in 1943, but it had no powers. By the end of the war women were no nearer equality with men in pay than they had been in 1939, unless they were on piece rates. That meant that they were paid for every item that they produced, and not for the number of hours that they worked. After the war, in 1946, a Royal Commission on Equal Pay reported that women should be given equal pay with men, but even this did not produce immediate results.

SOURCE D

The work that women are performing in munitions factories has to be seen to be believed. Precision engineering, which a few years ago would have made a skilled turner's hair stand on end, is now performed with dead accuracy by girls with no industrial experience.

Extract from a speech in the House of Commons made by Clement Attlee, Deputy Prime Minister, 1942.

SOURCE E

This war effort could not have been achieved if the women had not marched forward in millions and undertaken all kinds of tasks and work.

Winston Churchill, 1944.

Women in the armed forces

Women gradually began to play a more and more important role in the armed forces, especially after conscription was introduced in December 1941. By 1943 there were 443,000 women in the forces. They operated searchlights and barrage balloons and served in anti-aircraft batteries. In the navy they overhauled torpedoes and depth charges and repaired ships. As well as administrative tasks in the army, they also drove convoys, acted as despatch riders and worked in Intelligence.

Many of the code-breakers at Bletchley Park were women. In the Air Transport Auxiliary Service they flew planes to RAF bases.

Women in the voluntary services

Many women entered the voluntary services, although there was some opposition to them in 1939.

 **SOURCE F**

The Town Hall had objections. First they said they did not want any more women, and asked WHY I wanted to work when I was married. At length after four or five weeks they agreed to appoint me.

One woman's account of being turned down when first applying to be an ARP warden in December 1939.

As the war progressed, attitudes to women changed. In 1943 there were 180,000 women in the Civil Defence, which looked after local areas, and 47,000 in the fire services. Some 130,000 women served as messengers and despatch riders for the Post Office. Hundreds of thousands of others worked in auxiliary medical centres, first aid posts, mobile canteens and rest centres. Several million acted as fire-watchers who waited for incendiary bombs to fall and then tried to put out the fires that they started.

Women were not allowed to join the Home Guard, however, because people did not think that women should serve in the front line. Nevertheless many women took matters into their own hands and joined the Women's Home Defence Movement. They learnt how to handle firearms and prepare for an invasion.

The Land Army

The Land Army was revived in 1939 and altogether 80,000 women volunteered for work. British farming needed to produce as

SOURCE G

▲ A Land Army trainee spreading manure, November 1939.

much food as possible to try to prevent starvation as only about 45 per cent of Britain's food was home grown in 1939. During the war an extra 27 million acres were ploughed up for arable to make up the deficit.

Working as a 'land girl' was hard and some were badly treated (see Source H).

SOURCE H

In a large farm in Lincolnshire we worked for twelve hours a day at very hard and monotonous work and received no training. Wages were 28 shillings (£1.40) a week, out of which we had to pay £1 for our billets [lodgings]. At a smaller farm in Huntingdon, where we expected to be trained in tractor driving, we were made to do odd jobs, including kitchen work for the farmer's wife. The farmer gave us no training and refused to pay us any wages.

One woman's description of her work as a land girl in 1941.

Women in the home

In many ways the biggest challenge facing many women during the Second World War was making the rationing system work. No one ever went short of food, but coping with ration books and rations that could vary from week to week was a major task, especially in a large family.

An even bigger task was trying to provide some sort of variety in a diet that largely consisted of green vegetables, potatoes and bread. Manufacturers produced sauces, instant puddings and supplements to try to make the weekly rations look a little more appetising and go a little further. The government realised that food was very important to morale and the Ministry of Food

supplied hundreds of recipes. The first came out in 'Food Education Memos'. These advised the cook never to mention what was in the meal before it was eaten. For example:

- The ingredients of 'Hasty Pudding' were six tablespoons of oatmeal, three of suet, a pint of cold water and one onion. 'Mock Haggis' contained bacon rinds, oatmeal, bicarbonate of soda, one leek and vegetable water.

- Other recipes included Cabbage Soup, Cold Cream of Pea Soup (without cream), Fish and Leek Pudding, Sheep's Head Broth and Pig's Cheek Baked.

SOURCE I

Queuing became an obsession for some people. If one stopped in a shopping or market district to speak to a friend, one often found a queue forming. 'What are we queuing for?' was a common question.

One woman described how people were always on the look out for something extra.

Women were also asked to avoid all forms of waste. They were given instructions on how to cook when there was very little gas and what to do when there was an air raid (see Source K).

What was all the more remarkable was that the women who were coping with rationing were often the same women who were working during the day, doing voluntary work in the evenings and looking after their families. At the end of the war Winston Churchill admitted that without this unseen and unrecognised army of women, the war could easily have been lost. It is easy to count the numbers of women who served in the armed forces and

▲ Pamphlets supplied by the Ministry of Food in 1941, describing how to use rations effectively.

who volunteered for relief work during the war, but it is almost impossible to record the efforts of the millions of women who struggled to keep their households and families together year after year.

The arrival of US troops

The bombing of Pearl Harbor on 7 December 1941 brought the USA into the war and in January 1942 US troops began to arrive in Britain. Almost two million US troops, called GIs, as their uniforms were marked 'Government Issue', were stationed in Britain to prepare for the Allied invasion of Hitler's Europe.

Many of the GIs who came to Britain were part of the US airforce but many men were non-combat troops, in other words they were responsible for supplies of everything from vehicles and ammunition to clothing and food. The arrival of GIs had a huge impact on the British people who lived near the main US bases. Two of the bases were at Burtonwood and Warton in Lancashire, and the men

SOURCE K

If an air-raid signal takes you away from your kitchen for an indefinite time, the first thing to do is stop the heat; if you do this your food cannot get burnt, and we will tell you how to continue the cooking when you come back to the kitchen. An accident, a sudden call for help may call the housewife away from the stove.

Exract from a leaflet issued by the Ministry of Food, 1941.

stationed there spent much of their time off in the local towns and cities. The GIs were seen as glamorous and attractive by local people as they were relatively well paid and had smart uniforms. This gave rise to the saying that US troops were 'over-paid, over-sexed and over here'. In fact, some British women married GIs and many went to live with their husbands in the USA after the war.

The Beveridge Report

The impact of the war effort on the British people was far greater than anybody could have imagined in 1939. The experiences of the war, and rationing and evacuation, created a genuine desire to produce a new society in which the people of Britain were protected from the problems of poverty and ill health. The difficulties faced by many poor families in Britain had been highlighted in the Second Rowntree Report in 1936. Seebohm Rowntree had first reported on poverty thirty years before. Now he explained that many families still lived in poverty and that they were unable to help themselves. Government action was required if they were to live lives free from the disadvantages brought about by poverty.

The findings of the Second Rowntree report were later supported by the evidence of evacuation and rationing. These made it clear that not only could many poor families not afford a healthy diet, but that government intervention could also make a helpful difference. There was a strong feeling that the government not only had a responsibility to act, but that action could also be effective. In addition, German bombing had produced a housing crisis. With hundreds of thousands of homes destroyed or damaged, drastic action was going to be needed once the war was over. The housing crisis could not be left to chance or to private builders. Almost everyone agreed that the British people deserved better.

So, in 1941, in the middle of the Second World War, the British government asked Sir William Beveridge to lead a Royal Commission to consider how Britain should be rebuilt after the war. The Beveridge Report was published in 1942.

What did the Beveridge Report recommend?

The Beveridge Report recommended that the people of Britain should be protected from the Five Giant 'Evils': Squalor, Ignorance, Want, Idleness and Disease. It went on to explain how this could be done. Beveridge said that the government should take responsibility for the people of Britain, 'from the cradle to the grave'. He recommended that a welfare state should be set up in Britain.

Why did Beveridge recommend that a welfare state should be set up?

Beveridge had been involved in the Liberal reforms of the years from 1906 to 1914. However, these reforms had helped only a minority of people in Britain. The families of wage earners did not receive benefits and there was no automatic entitlement to medical treatment. Many mothers put off medical treatment for themselves in order to pay for treatment for their children.

The Second Rowntree Report in 1936 had shown that poverty still existed in Britain and about ten per cent of the population suffered real hardship. In addition the suffering of the British people during the war convinced many politicians that real action must be taken.

The evidence from the evacuation showed just what the lives of some people in Britain were like. Many evacuees were in very poor health (see pages 5–6). Rationing showed that government intervention could be effective.

On publication in October 1942, the Beveridge Report became a best-seller and the British government committed itself to setting up a welfare state as soon as the war ended.

The Butler Education Act, 1944

The first part of the welfare state was put into place in 1944. The coalition government passed the Butler Education Act, which was based on the Hadow Report of 1926 and the Spens Report of 1938.

The Butler Education Act tackled one of Beveridge's Five Giant 'Evils': Ignorance. It immediately suggested that the government should give education greater priority. All fees for state schools were abolished and it suggested that the school leaving age was raised to fifteen.

In future, all children would attend secondary schools for the first time. They would go to primary schools from the ages of five to eleven and then to secondary schools from the ages of eleven to fifteen. At the age of eleven, all children would take a test, the '11 plus', to decide what form of secondary education was appropriate for them. There were to be three types of schools: Grammar, Secondary Modern and Technical. All three types of schools were to enjoy equal status and equal resources.

The 1944 Act marked an important change in educational policy in Britain. For the first time the government acknowledged that all children had a right to secondary education free of charge.

The end of the war

The last German troops surrendered to the Allies on 7 May 1945. During the war, party politics had taken a back seat because all three political parties had been involved in a coalition government. However, Winston Churchill had said that a general election would be held as soon as the war was over. This took place in July 1945.

While people admired Churchill and his achievements in leading Britain to victory in the war, they were concerned about his ability to improve life for people in Britain after the war. Churchill lost the election and was replaced by the Labour politician, Clement Attlee. The Labour Party won the election partly because it promised to set up the welfare state, which had been outlined in the Beveridge Report in 1942. The Labour Party promised to do more to help the ordinary people of Britain who had suffered so much and immediately began to plan the rest of the welfare state.

In 1945 there was a real determination that the sacrifices of the last six years' fighting should not have been in vain. The end of the war was greeted with great relief and rejoicing, but also with a belief that a better world must come out of the chaos and destruction. The plans set out in the Beveridge Report suggested that something would be done in 1945.

But for some of the people who had given so much to the war effort, peacetime proved to be something of a disappointment.

Attempts were now made to persuade women to give up their jobs. The reason for this policy was very simple. As the war came to an end, women were sacked so that men could get their jobs back. All over the country, women were dismissed after years of hard work.

SOURCE A

There were twelve women welders in the yard at the time and we were sent for one morning and the personnel officer sat there at his desk. He lifted his head and he said one word 'redundant'. That was a new word in our vocabulary. We really didn't know exactly what it meant. There was no reason given. There was no explanation. There was plenty of work in the yard.

The experience of a woman welder in a shipyard at the end of the war.

All kinds of advertisements put pressure on women to go back to the home, just as they had put pressure on women to volunteer and to be careful and not waste anything for the last six years. When women went to Labour Exchanges (the forerunners of job centres), they found that the chances of getting a job were slim. The government stated that men should have priority over women for all jobs. It was certainly the case that women who wanted to work full time found themselves discriminated against in the years after the war.

SOURCE B

Oh my goodness, you've got the best qualifications that we've ever had that's applied for a job. But you are a woman, and I wonder what the boys would say if I employed a woman.

An employer's reason for dismissing a woman who had been a welder during the war.

This policy was supported by many employers. Men who returned from the armed forces were given priority over women who had worked in war factories. Although girls now had equality with men in education, in theory at least, that equality was not put into practice in the workplace.

SOURCE C

It is doubtless true that there are many jobs done during the war by women for which men are better suited, both mentally and physically. And, if there is to be a nation in the future, there must be children and children mean homes and endless chores. So that there must naturally be a drift back from the services and the factories to domestic work.

Extract from a statement issued by the Ministry of Information in 1945.

Sample coursework assignment

SOURCE A

From *Waiting for the All Clear*, a book published in 1990 to mark the fiftieth anniversary of the Blitz. This extract comes from the publisher's description of the book's contents inside the front cover.

Fifty years ago during the Blitz, the British people showed that they didn't have to be in uniform to be heroes. Out of terror and tragedy came courage and an unshakeable determination. Those at home in the most appalling circumstances kept their sense of humour. Their memories will break your heart and make you smile.

SOURCE B

▲ A photograph dated 21 January 1943. In the air raid of 20 January on London, Catford Girls School was hit. Photographs which had anything to do with the war had to be approved before they could be published. This photograph showing bodies in sacking was banned by the censors.

▲ A photograph published in October 1940. It was published with the caption 'Homeless but not downhearted: three generations on the move in London.'

▲ This photograph was taken on 16 November 1940 after the air raid on Coventry. It shows gutted buildings and debris in Hertford Street.

SOURCE E

Extract from a secret report to the government by the Ministry of Information, 10 September 1940.

When the siren goes, people run madly for shelters. Citizens' Advice Bureau is inundated [swamped] with mothers and young children hysterical and asking to be removed from the district. Exodus [flight] from the East End growing rapidly. Taxi drivers report taking group after group to Euston* and Paddington* with belongings.

*Euston and Paddington are London railway stations

SOURCE F

From Harold Nicolson's diary, 17 September 1940. Harold Nicolson knew several members of the government.

Everyone is worried about the feeling in the East End of London where there is much bitterness. It is said that even the king and queen were booed the other day when they visited the destroyed areas.

SOURCE G

From the book *Don't you Know There's A War On?* published in 1988.

As long as there were men and women to continue production, the country's economic life could continue and the planes, tanks and armaments roll off the assembly lines. Attendance at work remained surprisingly good.

Understandably there was widespread fear during the Blitz. This frequently led to flights of entire communities into the countryside, or 'trekking' as it was called at the time. So Londoners escaped to Epping Forest during the bombing of the East End. Yet many of those who trekked were the same people who continued to turn up for work.

? Assignment One: Objective 1

1. Why were the major cities of Britain bombed by the Germans in 1940–1? **(15)**

2. Describe the effects of the Blitz on everyday life in Britain. **(15)**

3. In what ways did the British government attempt to hide the effects of the Blitz from the people of Britain? **(20)**

(Total: 50 marks)

? Assignment Two: Objectives 2 and 3

1. Study Source A. What can you learn from Source A about the response of the British people to the effects of the Blitz? **(6)**

2. Study Sources B and C. How useful are Sources B and C in helping you to understand the effects of the Blitz on people in Britain? **(10)**

3. Study Sources B, C and D. Does Source D support the evidence of Sources B and C about the damage done during air raids? **(8)**

4. Study Sources E, F and G. Use Sources E, F and G, and your own knowledge, to explain why the government was concerned about the morale (spirit and attitude) of the British people in the autumn of 1940. **(12)**

5. Study all the sources, and use your own knowledge.

   The impression that the British faced the Blitz with courage and unity is a myth.

   Use the sources, and your own knowledge, to explain whether you agree with this statement. **(14)**

(Total: 50 marks)